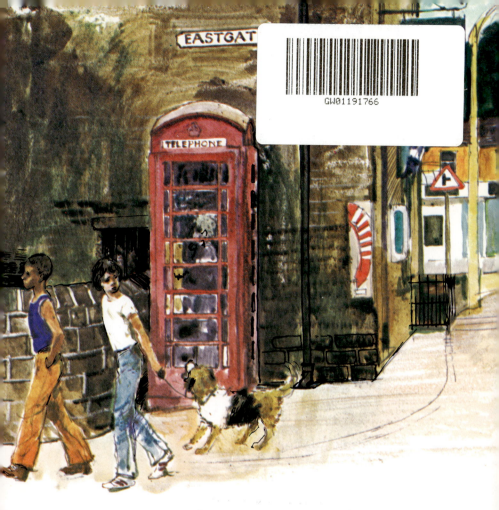

Jim and John were going past a telephone box.
Boy barked.
"What's the matter, Boy?" said John.

Someone slipped out of the box
and ran off down the road.
No wonder Boy barked.
It was Mark Fox!

"Look," said Jim.
"A fire engine!"
"Come on, John.
Let's follow it."

The fire engine raced past.
Then it stopped at a house
not far from the phone.
John and Jim were soon there.
But where was the fire?

Firemen ran into the house.
Then they ran out again.
The Fire Chief was very angry.
"That's four false alarms this week!" he shouted.

The Fire Chief
walked up to John and Jim.
"These false alarms," he said.
"Do you know anything
about them?"

"No," said John.
"But we will try and find out."
"Good," said the Fire Chief.
He looked at them hard.

Boy barked.
He pulled at his lead.
"Now what's the matter?" said John.
He looked up and saw Mark Fox,
peeping round the corner.
Then Mark ran away.

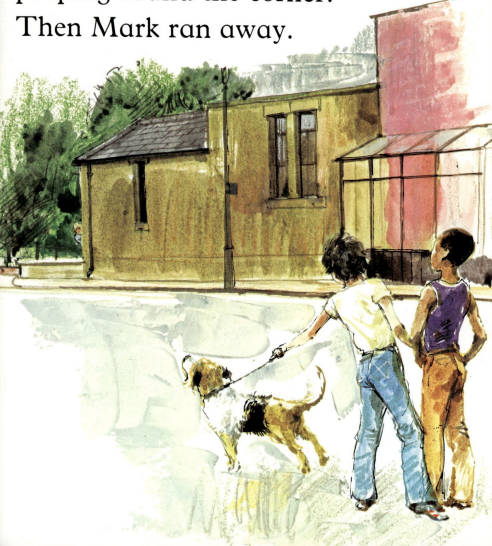

That night,
John thought hard.
What was Mark doing
in that phone box?
Why did he run away?
Had Mark called the fire brigade?

Next day he talked to Jim.
"It must be Mark," Jim said.
"All right, then," John said.
"Let's hide by that phone box and see if he phones again."

So they hid.
Nothing happened.
Nothing at all.
"Oh let's go home,"
said Jim at last.
"Sshhhh!" said John.
"Someone's coming."

An old woman went into the box. She talked and talked. That wasn't a false alarm!
"Let's go home," said Jim again.

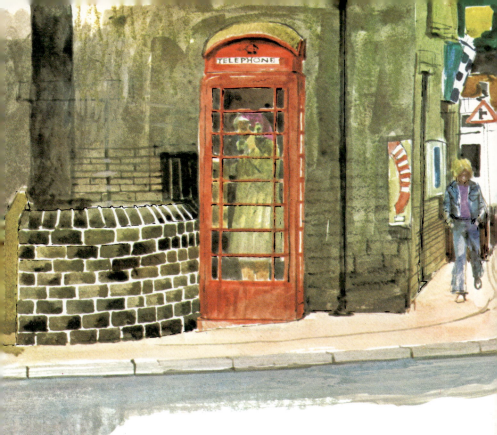

But someone else
was coming now.
Boy growled softly.
"Quiet!" said John.
But Boy was right.
This time it was
Mark Fox!

Mark waited for
the old woman to go.
He looked up the road.
He looked down the road.
Then he went into the box.

John could just see
his finger on the dial.
He dialled nine . . .
nine . . . nine!

Mark slipped out
of the phone box.
He was grinning.
They saw him hide
round the corner.

The fire engine
raced up to a shop.
"There's no fire here,"
shouted the Fire Chief.
"Another false alarm!"

John shouted at Mark.
"You called the fire engine, didn't you?"
Mark turned and ran.
"After him!" shouted John.

Mark ran so fast
that John and Jim lost him.
But Boy kept up.
John heard him barking.
"That way!" he shouted.

They turned a corner.
There was Boy, barking.
And there was Mark Fox.
The road was a dead end.
Boy had trapped him!

Mark picked up a big stick.
Slowly he came towards Boy.
"Get out of my way," he said.
But Boy did not move.

Suddenly!
The fire engine raced up.
Woosh! Splosh! Splash!
A jet of water hit Mark!

The Fire Chief grabbed him.
"Got you at last," he said.
Mark looked wet
and very, very scared.

The Fire Chief turned to John and Jim.
"If dogs were firemen, I'd make Boy a Chief!"